Nature's Children

LLAMAS

Amanda Harman

GROLIER

5050 30 10 7 55835

FACTS IN BRIEF

Classification of Llamas

Class: *Mammalia* (mammals)
Order: *Artiodactyla* (even-toed hoofed mammals)
Suborder: *Tylopoda* (camels and llamas)
Family: *Camelidae* (camels and llamas)
Genus: *Lama*
Species: *Lama glama*

World distribution.   The Andes Mountains in South America in Peru, Bolivia, Chile, and Argentina; also introduced into the United States, Canada, Australia, and Europe.

Habitat.   Mountain grasslands and shrublands.

Distinctive physical characteristics.   Fairly tall and graceful, with a long neck and snout; divided top lip; long, thick hair on neck and body with shorter hair on head and lower legs.

Habits.   Lives in herds of females with one male. Feeds during the day and rests at night.

Diet.   Vegetation such as leaves, small twigs, and grasses.

© 2004 The Brown Reference Group plc
Printed and bound in U.S.A.
Edited by John Farndon and Angela Koo

Published by:

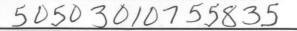

GROLIER

**An imprint of Scholastic
Library Publishing
Old Sherman Turnpike, Danbury,
Connecticut 06816**

Library of Congress Cataloging-in-Publication Data
Harman, Amanda, 1968–
  Llamas / Amanda Harman.
    p. cm. — (Nature's children)
  Includes index.
  Summary: Describes the physical characteristics, habits, and habitats of llamas.
  ISBN 0–7172–5957–9 (set)   ISBN 0–7172–5968–4
    1. Llamas—Juvenile literature. [1. Llamas.] I. Title. II. Series.

  QL737.U54H37 2004
  599.63'67—dc22

                     2003049172

Contents

Llamas look a lot like small, shaggy camels and seem to look down their nose at you. They sometimes even kick out or spit at people or other animals that threaten them. But if you look after them well and take the chance to get to know them, they are very gentle and friendly creatures.

Llamas have been very important farm animals for thousands of years in South America, where they originally come from. They provide meat and wool for their owners and can be trained to carry heavy loads or pull carts. In some parts of the world they even guard sheep.

The natural home of llamas is high up in the Andes Mountains of South America.

Big and Woolly

Opposite page:
A llama's curled top lip helps it twist off plants to eat.

Llamas are large four-legged creatures with thick, woolly coats. The biggest llamas are around 8 feet (2.5 meters) long from the tip of their tails to the top of their heads. They are about 4 feet (1.2 meters) tall at the shoulder too, so they can easily look down their nose at you. Most are whitish, but they can be all kinds of colors. Some are brown. Some are black. Some are gray. Some are honey colored.

A llama's head is surprisingly small for such a large creature. And it is perched on top of a very, very long neck. A llama also has huge dark eyes and long, elegant eyelashes, as well as large, pointed, upright ears. Its top lip curls down a little at the front. That is to help it twist off plants when eating, but it gives the llama a very snooty look!

Unlike most other hoofed animals, llamas run by pacing—moving both legs on the same side together.

On the Hoof

Llamas are hoofed animals. That means they have hooves on the ends of their legs, like most big four-legged animals that eat grass. Horses, cows, and sheep all have hooves. A hoof is actually a kind of toe. But it is covered in a hard, protective material—the same material that toenails are made from. Most hoofed animals walk directly on their hooves, but llamas' hooves don't quite touch the ground. Instead, llamas walk on a tough, leathery sole that sticks out below the hoof. These pads don't slip like hooves and make llamas very sure-footed when clambering around their rocky mountain home.

Llamas are unlike other hoofed animals in the way they run too. Most hoofed animals move the legs on the same side alternately, but llamas move both legs on the same side together. This unusual way of moving is called "pacing." It makes llamas rock from side to side, but they look very graceful as they move.

Camel Cousins

Llamas originally came from South America, but they have some cousins across the other side of the world in Africa and Asia: camels. Camels have the same long necks and the same split upper lip that gives them the same snooty expression. Like llamas, they also have just two toes on each foot, which is unusual among four-legged animals. Like llamas, too, they are mostly domesticated and used as pack animals. But while llamas are used to living in high mountains where it is cold and windy, camels live in very hot, dry places. In fact, some live right in the middle of the Sahara Desert in Africa.

Camels have a number of features that help them deal with deserts. The most amazing feature is the big hump of fat on their back. Dromedary camels from Africa and the Middle East have one hump. Bactrian camels from Asia have two. The hump provides the camel with a supply of extra food when times are hard.

The Llama Family

Llamas have three close South American mountain relatives: the vicuna, the alpaca, and the guanaco. Together they make up what scientists call the lamoid (said LAH-moyd) family. Like the llama, all of these creatures have been tamed at one time or another, so it is hard to say which is wild and which isn't.

The llama's closest relative is the guanaco (said gwa-NAH-co). The llama is actually a domesticated form of the guanaco. The guanaco lives in the Andes Mountains and on South America's grassy plains in groups of up to 122 animals. It runs fast and is a good swimmer. It shares an unusual ability with camels: It can kneel on its front knees.

Vicuna (said vik-OON-ya) are dainty versions of guanacos that live on the highest slopes of the Andes, grazing on grass. They are now very rare in the wild. Alpacas are, like llamas, tame descendants of guanacos. But while llamas were bred to carry things, alpacas were bred for their long, soft wool.

Opposite page:
Llamas are related to smaller guanacos, which still live wild in some parts of the Andes Mountains.

13

High Home

Llamas once lived only in the high mountains of the Andes, especially in Peru, Bolivia, Chile, and Argentina. With their warm, shaggy coats, strong legs, sure feet, and unbeatable stamina they make the perfect pack animal for the people who live there and travel along the narrow mountain paths. They feed quite happily on the short, stubby grass that grows on high plains and slopes between 10,000 and 16,400 feet up (3,000 to 5,000 meters).

Llamas are easy to keep and very adaptable, however. So in recent years people have taken them all around the world, mainly to breed them for their coarse wool. You can now see herds of llamas on farms in Canada, Australia, and the United States. They are particularly tolerant of the tough grass that many other grazing animals turn up their noses at.

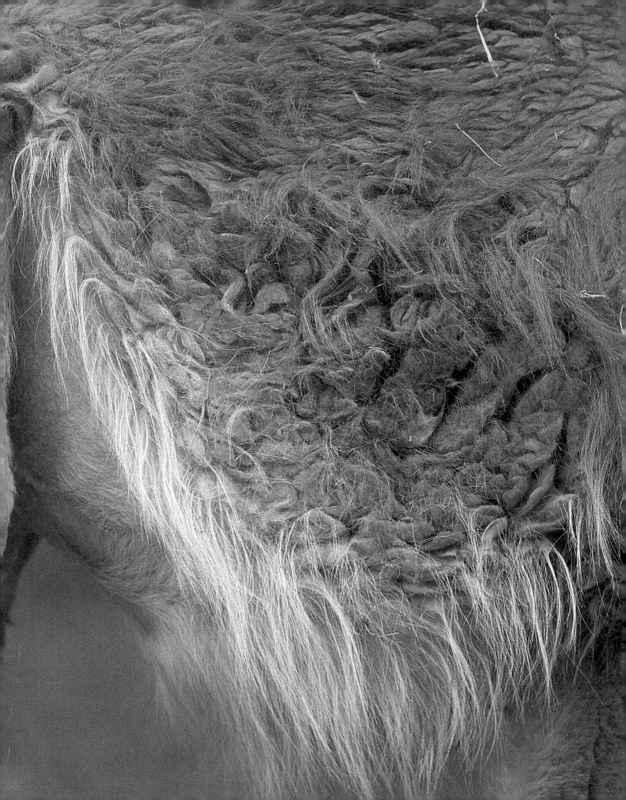

Snuggly Coat

Mountain plains are harsh, unwelcoming places. It is cold high up on the hillsides, and the country is wide open to the wind and the freezing rain. Llamas are perfectly at home there, however. They have thick hair that keeps them snug on colder days and during the night. It also keeps them cool on warm days.

The llamas' dense coat is made up of two layers. On the outside the animals are protected from the rain by a layer of straight hairs up to 10 inches (25 centimeters) long. Underneath, a layer of shorter wavy hairs keeps the cold out and the warmth in. When people keep llamas in warm places like Florida, they have to cut the animals' fur in summer to allow them to stay cool.

A llama's amazingly thick coat keeps it warm and dry in the cold, rainy mountains.

Thin Air, Dry Soil

Mountains are not only cold. They are tough places to live because the air is very thin too. That means the air contains much less oxygen than it does lower down. Animals need to breathe plenty of oxygen to keep their bodies going. Without enough oxygen most animals would get weak and ill. But llamas have special blood that helps them thrive in thin air. Guanacos, alpacas, and vicunas have the same special blood.

Mountain plains are also very dry. Many animals cannot live in such dry places because they need to find fresh water to drink every day. Llamas can survive for several days without drinking because they get most of the water they need from the plants they eat.

There is not much to drink in the mountains, but llamas can get their water from the plants they eat.

Llamas and the Incas

Llamas were among the first animals in the world to be tamed. They were tamed by the Incas. The Incas were a group of South American Indians. They set up a mighty empire in the Andes Mountains many thousands of years ago. Around 4,000 years ago, in a place near Lake Titicaca between Bolivia and Peru, the Incas tamed some wild guanacos. They began to breed the animals and use them for meat and for carrying heavy loads. Taking wild animals and breeding tame ones from them is called domestication.

Eventually, after thousands of years of breeding, the animal that the Incas tamed became different from the wild guanaco. This animal was the llama. So llamas have never existed in the wild. Today they still live only with humans as farm animals or pets.

Opposite page:
The Indians of the mountains of Peru and Bolivia have reared llamas for thousands of years.

Beasts of Burden

Llamas are particularly useful to people in the Andes because they can thrive in the high mountains. They are also gentle animals that get on surprisingly well with humans and do not panic easily.

In the past llamas were most valuable as pack animals. Pack animals carry heavy loads of goods and materials from one place to another. So, sometimes llamas are known as "beasts of burden." A healthy, fully grown llama can carry over 100 pounds (45 kilograms) on its back. It can also carry that weight over difficult ground high up in the mountains for around 18 miles (29 kilometers) a day. That was once very useful for carrying things along mountain tracks too narrow for carts. Since cars and trucks have been invented, though, llamas have become less popular as pack animals.

Stubborn Creatures

Although llamas are no longer used much
for practical transportation, tourists can hire
llamas to carry their belongings and picnics
on walks. Llamas can even give children rides,
although they are not strong enough to carry
adults. And they can be used to carry
equipment and supplies for park rangers
or on hunting and fishing expeditions along
paths cars and trucks can't get to.

Llamas can be very stubborn when they
want to be. If you try to load a pack onto one
llama, it will probably refuse to go anywhere.
It may even lie down on the ground, hissing
and spitting—especially if the pack is too
heavy. But if you treat it well and load it up
in a group of other llamas, you will have no
problems. Llamas can even be taught to walk
in a long line, each one joined to the pack
on the llama in front by a string.

25

Farm Animals and Pets

Llamas are sometimes farmed for their meat and their wool. Llama meat is particularly popular among the peoples in the Andes. Llama wool is produced in Australia, New Zealand, and some parts of Europe. Llamas are usually sheared every two years. Each llama produces around 7 pounds (over 3 kilograms) of wool. The wool is woven together to make all kinds of goods, such as rugs, blankets, ponchos, scarves, and hats. The long, coarse outer hair is often used to make rope.

In the United States llamas are very popular as pets and show animals. They are so intelligent that they can be taught to pull carts—even over, around, and through obstacles in competitions. Well-trained llamas are also unafraid of large crowds and are often used for children's parties and big parades.

Opposite page: *People who live in the Andes spin the soft wool of llamas to make clothes and rugs.*

Friendly Llamas

Llamas are very sociable animals. They like to live together in a herd. Each herd is made up of one male, several females, and their youngsters. The male is the overall leader of the herd, but there is a boss female, too, who tells the other females what to do.

Llamas spend the daytime roaming the mountainsides in their herds, browsing and grazing. As they go, they let each other know where they are and if they are safe. They do this by making sounds and moving their neck, ears, and tail in certain ways. At night the llamas sleep, lying down on the ground.

Llamas are surprisingly friendly animals and may greet each other by rubbing their necks together.

Fighting for the Herd

Male llamas are very protective of their herds of females. They set up their own chosen patch of land, or territory, and constantly try to keep other male llamas out of it. To let other males know they are there, they leave piles of dung around the edges of the territory.

If another male enters the territory, the herd's male attacks him viciously. Male llamas have six sharp, hooked fighting teeth at the back of their mouths. They develop when they are around three years old. They try to use these teeth to bite and wound each other's legs.

Male llamas don't like any other males coming onto their patch. Any male that dares to wander in is quickly chased away.

Guard Llamas

Opposite page: *Male llamas are so good at protecting their patch that farmers often get them to protect their flocks of sheep.*

One advantage of living in a herd is that llamas can help each other look out for predators. If one spots danger, it makes a high-pitched alarm call. The other llamas then quickly run away. The llama's main predator is the puma, a wildcat also called the cougar. Another potential enemy is packs of wild dogs called "coyotes." Male llamas don't always run when they spot a predator. Sometimes they try to kick them and chase them away.

In fact, llamas are so good at protecting each other that people often use them to guard their flocks of sheep. They may even be used to guard herds of deer and cattle or flocks of geese and ducks. The male or female llama is kept together with the flock just as if it was one of them. A single llama can protect as many as 2,000 sheep.

As you can see, the grass of the high Andes Mountains is pretty rough, so llamas have to eat a lot to keep well fed.

A Mountain of Food

Llamas are herbivores, or plant-eaters. They like to reach into trees and shrubs to eat leaves and small twigs. This is called browsing. Llamas also graze on grasses and other low plants. Some farmers feed their llamas on hay and occasionally treat them to fruit and vegetables like apples, carrots, and broccoli.

In the South American mountains most of the plant material that the llamas feed on is not very nutritious. This means that the llamas and other herbivores that live there have to eat a lot of it to get enough energy.

Chewing the Cud

Opposite page:
The plants a llama eats are so tough it has to chew and swallow them— then bring them up partly digested and chew them again!

Plants are very difficult to break down, or digest. Llamas have big side teeth with raised edges for crushing tough plant material. Even so, they have to chew their food for a long time. First it goes into the stomach to be digested a little. Then it comes back up into the mouth so that the llamas can chew some more. The softened food from the stomach is called a cud, and we say that llamas "chew the cud." Sometimes this can look as though they are thinking carefully and chewing gum. Llamas chew the cud for more than seven hours a day. When the food has been chewed enough, it goes back down into another part of the stomach to be digested even more!

Baby Crias

In South America the mating season for llamas is in August and September. This means that when babies are born one year later, it is summer, and there is plenty of food available for the mother. This means that she is able to produce all the milk her young baby needs. Female llamas give birth every two years, usually to just one baby at a time.

A baby llama is called a cria. Crias weigh between 20 and 35 pounds (9 and 15 kilograms) when they are born. They can stand up and move around within a half hour. They are very hungry and start to feed on their mother's milk right away.

This little cria (baby llama) is standing on its own legs, but it is less than 18 hours old.

Growing Up

By the time crias are eight months old, they stop drinking their mother's milk and feed totally on plant material. At this point the adult male of the herd chases the young males away so that they can go and find herds of their own. Young llamas have milk teeth at first. They drop out, and new adult teeth grow when the llamas are about two years old.

Male llamas are old enough to set up and defend their own herds when they are between four and five years old. Until then they form small groups called "bachelor bands." They practice play fighting in preparation for the future, when they will have to do it for real.

When they are young, llamas have much shorter, downier fur and a shorter snout.

All Grown-up

Adult llamas are all different sizes. When they are fully grown, the smallest ones weigh around 225 pounds (105 kilograms), and the largest ones weigh around 450 pounds (205 kilograms). That means that some big llamas are as heavy as three adult humans.

Llamas are old enough to mate and have crias of their own when they are between one and two years old. Llamas, guanacos, alpacas, and vicunas are all so closely related that they can mate with each other and produce healthy babies. People in the Middle East have even been able to breed a llama and a camel together. The baby of a llama and a camel is called a camma.

Adult llamas are surpisingly varied in size. In one group you may find some twice as big as others.

Vicuna Loss

Opposite page:
*It once seemed
as if wild vicunas
would be killed
off by hunting.
But they have
been saved by
conservation
efforts.*

There are now about four million llamas
around the world; but their little cousin, the
vicuna, was once much, much rarer. During
the time of the Incas a million or more
vicunas roamed the Andes. But after the
Spanish conquerors arrived here some 500
years ago, vicunas were hunted mercilessly
for their beautiful cinnamon-colored fleece
(woolly coat). By the 1960s there were just
10,000 left in the world.

In a desperate effort to save the vicuna, the
Peruvian government encouraged local people
to shear the wool from the vicunas. If they had
no fleece, they thought, hunters would not
want to kill them. The fleeces could also be
sold to help the poor villagers. The plan was
so successful that by 2002 there were over a
quarter of a million vicunas in the wild.

Woolly Alpacas

Like llamas, alpacas are kept by people and don't live in the wild. You can see their herds grazing in the mountain forests and plains of Peru, Bolivia, Argentina, and Chile. Just as the llama was domesticated from the wild guanaco, scientists now think the alpaca was originally domesticated from the wild vicuna.

The alpaca has a thicker and silkier coat than the llama. That keeps it very warm and means that it can survive even when the temperature drops to $-18°C$ ($0°F$). Because of its thickness people value alpaca wool even more than llama wool. The alpaca is now the most important farm animal in South America.

Words to Know

Breed To produce young.

Cud Partly digested food bought up from the stomach to the mouth to chew again by grazing animals such as cows.

Digest To break down food so that an animal's body can get at the important parts it needs to survive.

Domestication The taming and breeding of an animal or plant to live with humans and be useful to them.

Herbivore An animal that eats only plants, not meat.

Lamoid Llama, alpaca, guanaco, and vicuna.

Mammal Any warm-blooded animal that is covered by hair or fur, gives birth to live young, and makes milk to feed them.

Mate To come together to produce young.

Nutritious Describing food that provides animals with ingredients they need to survive.

Oxygen A gas in the air that animals breathe in and use in their bodies.

Predator An animal that hunts and eats other animals for food.

Species A particular type of animal.

Territory An area where an animal hunts or breeds. The animal generally defends its territory against other animals.

Ungulate A mammal that has hooves.

INDEX

Cover Photo: Oxford Scientific Films: Mark Jones
Photo Credits: Ardea: John Daniels 16, 41, Kenneth W. Fink 37, François Gohier 4, 8, 29, 38; Bruce Coleman: Robert Maier 7, Hans Reinhard 12; NHPA: G. I. Bernard 19, Joe Blossom 33, Kevin Schafer 45; Oxford Scientific Films: Doug Allan 34, David Cayless 11, Daniel Cox 15, Patti Murray 42; Still Pictures: Julio Etchart 24/25, John Isaac 26, Mike Kolloffel 20.